discover  countries

Nigeria

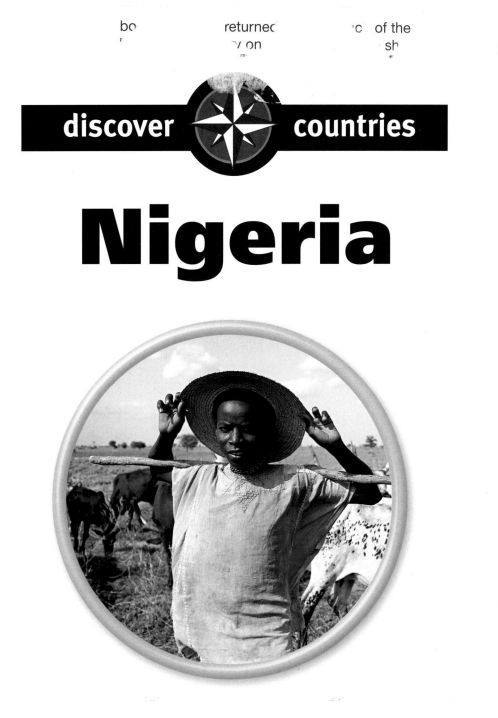

Ali Brownlie Bojang

WAYLAND

Published in paperback in 2014 by Wayland
Copyright Wayland 2014

Wayland
Hachette Children's Books
338 Euston Road
London NW1 3BH

Wayland Australia
Level 17/207 Kent Street,
Sydney, NSW 2000

Concept design: Jason Billin
Editor: Susan Crean
Designer: Amy Sparks
Consultant: Rob Bowden

Produced for Wayland by
White-Thomson Publishing Ltd

www.wtpub.co.uk
+44 (0)845 362 8240

British Library Cataloguing in Publication Data

Bojang, Ali Brownlie

Nigeria - (Discover countries)

1. Nigeria-Juvenile literature

I. Title II. Series

966.9'054-dc22

ISBN-13: 9780750280907

Printed in China
2 4 6 8 10 9 7 5 3 1
Wayland is a division of Hachette Children's Books
an Hachette UK company
www.hachette.co.uk

All data in this book was researched in 2009
and has been collected from the latest sources available at that time.

Picture credits
1, WTPix; 3 Shutterstock/Francois van der Merwe (top), Shutterstock/Lydia Kruger (bottom); 4 (map), Stefan Chabluk; 5, Corbis/Wolfgang Kumm/dpa; 6, iStock/Klaas Lingbeek; 7, Shutterstock/Francois van der Merwe; 8, WTPix; 9, WTPix; 10, WTPix; 11, Photoshot/Eye Ubiquitous; 12, Corbis/Lawrence Manning; 13, Shutterstock/Lydia Kruger; 14, Photoshot/Eye Ubiquitous; 15, Corbis/Ankitunde Akinleye/Reuters; 16, Corbis/Paul Almasy; 17, Photoshot/Eye Ubiquitous; 18, Photoshot/WpN;19, WTPix; 20, Photoshot; 21, WTPix; 22, WTPix; 23, Corbis/James Marshall; 24, Corbis/Ed Kashi; 25 Corbis/Daniel Lainé; 26, Shutterstock/Jonathan Larsen; 27 Corbis/George Esiri/Reuters; 28, Photoshot/Eye Ubiquitous; 29, Corbis/Ed Kashi
Front cover images, Corbis/Wolfgang Kumm/dpa (left), WTPix (right)

Contents

Discovering Nigeria

Although Nigeria is the fourteenth largest of Africa's 59 countries, it has the most people. Nigeria's population of 150 million means that one in five Africans are Nigerian. The country also has valuable oil resources and a powerful army. For these reasons, Nigeria is known as the 'Giant of Africa'.

From ancient kingdoms to independence

The history of the people who lived in the land that is now Nigeria goes back 10,000 years. More than 250 different ethnic groups settled and now live in Nigeria, and many of its kingdoms and empires have flourished and faded away.

One of the most famous of these was the Benin Kingdom, which was powerful around the fifteenth century. During this time European traders, including the British, arrived in the region and eventually established the slave trade.

DID YOU KNOW?

The colour green in the national flag of Nigeria represents the land and the richness of the soil. The colour white represents peace and harmony.

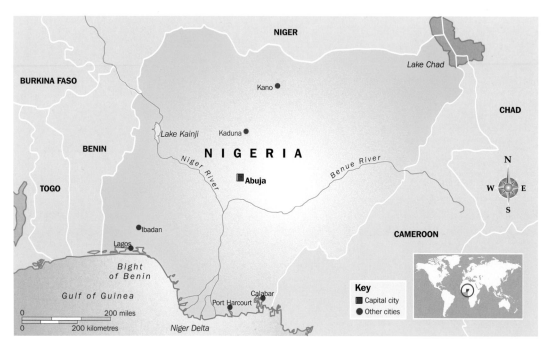

Enslaved Africans were taken to European colonies in the Caribbean and North America. The British stopped trading slaves in 1807. In the nineteenth century Nigeria became a British colony until the country gained its independence in 1960.

Since independence

For many years after it became independent, Nigeria was ruled by force under an army. In 1999 Nigeria became a democracy headed by a president, and the people were able to vote for their rulers.

Nigeria has 36 states, each with its own government that makes decisions about how to run its own affairs. The country is generally peaceful. However, there are long-lasting rivalries between different ethnic groups and religions, and between people in the north and the south of Nigeria, which has sometimes flared up in violence.

⬥ Abuja was planned as Nigeria's capital and most of it was built in the 1980s. The central mosque was one of the new city's first buildings.

Nigeria Statistics

Area: 923,768 sq km (356,669 sq miles)

Capital city: Abuja

Government type: Republic

Bordering countries: Cameroon, Chad, Niger, Benin

Currency: Naira

Language: English (official). Hausa, Yoruba, Ibo, Fulani and 300 local languages.

Landscape and climate

Nigeria has varied landscapes, from tropical beaches and forests to deserts. With an average temperature of 23-32°C (73-90°F), everywhere is hot all year round. Nigeria's seasons are based on whether or not they are rainy, rather than whether they are hot or cold.

The coastal area

About one-third of Nigeria's coast is a long line of sandy beaches. The Niger Delta, one of the largest wetland areas in the world, occupies the rest of the coastline. The Niger Delta is where the River Niger spreads out into a maze of streams and creeks where it meets the sea. It is here where most of Nigeria's oil is found. Further inland, there is higher land covered with thick rainforest.

Nigeria's coastal region has the country's highest rainfall, at around 2,000 mm (80 inches). This falls in two rainy seasons – a long one from March to July and a short one from September to October.

Central Nigeria

The central region is not as hot as the north or as humid as the south. It is an area of grasslands and open woodland. The annual rainfall in this area is between 500-1,500 mm (20-60 inches).

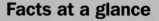

Facts at a glance

Land area: 910,768 sq km (351,649 sq miles)

Water area: 13,000 sq km (5,019 sq miles)

Highest point: Chappal Waddi, 2,419 m (7,936 ft)

Lowest point: Atlantic Ocean, 0 m

Longest river: River Niger 4,180 km (2,597 miles)

Coastline: 853 km (530 miles)

⭕ Pools and waterfalls like Gurara Falls, near Abuja, are created where streams flow over rocks.

The north

The tropical grasslands continue north from central Nigeria. Total rainfall decreases as you move north and the landscape becomes drier. In the very far north it turns into desert. Temperatures can reach 45°C (113°F), and the area often suffers from droughts. For five months of the year, from November to April, there is no rain.

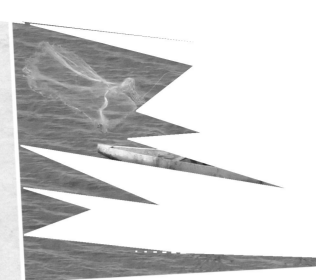

Rivers and mountains

The Niger River and its tributaries are vital to many communities across Nigeria. The waters from the rivers mean that farmers can grow crops and people have water for drinking and washing.

Nigeria's highest mountains are in the east. Nigeria's highest point — Chappal Waddi, at 2,419 m (7,936 ft) – is found here.

A changing climate

Climate change has already affected Nigeria. An increase of rainfall in the south has led to increased incidents of flooding. A decrease of rainfall in the north has led to the spread of deserts further into Nigeria from the Sahara desert.

⬤ The River Niger and its tributaries cover two-thirds of the country. Many people in Nigeria depend on them for their livelihood.

DID YOU KNOW? In the dry season, the *Harmattan* wind blows across Nigeria bringing sand and dust from the Sahara Desert as far south as Lagos. It can reduce visibility so much that planes have to be diverted!

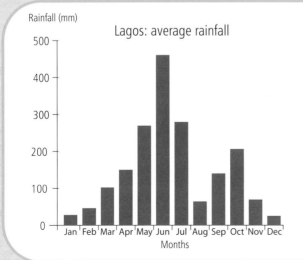

Rainfall (mm)
Lagos: average rainfall
Months

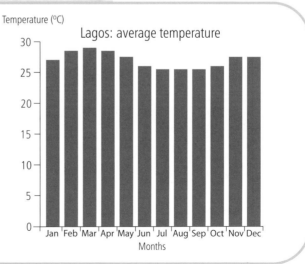

Temperature (°C)
Lagos: average temperature
Months

Population and health

With a population of 170 million people, Nigeria has the seventh largest population in the world. Yet despite having many resources, more than 70 per cent of Nigerians live in poverty. This means they live on less than US$1 a day, making Nigeria one of the poorest countries in the world.

Nigeria's people

There are more than 250 different ethnic groups in Nigeria. The Fulani people are an ethnic group spread throughout much of West Africa. In Nigeria, they have absorbed much of the Hausa language and culture. The Hausa and Fulani ethnic groups mainly live in the north, while the Yoruba live in the south. The Igbos live mainly in the south-east. None of the three main ethnic groups makes up a majority and the population is fairly evenly split between Muslims and Christians.

Facts at a glance

Total population:
170 million

Life expectancy at birth:
52.05 years

Children dying before the age of five: 19.1%

Ethnic composition: More than 250 ethnic groups, including: Hausa and Fulani 29%, Yoruba 21%, Igbo (Ibo) 18%, Ijaw 10%, Kanuri 4%, Ibibio 3.5%, Tiv 2.5%

▼ Children are highly valued in Nigeria, and over 40 per cent of Nigerians are under the age of 14.

A population strain

Nigeria's population is one of the fastest growing in the world. One of the reasons for this is that children are highly valued amongst all the different ethnic groups. However, the country's large population puts a great strain on Nigeria's resources. It is difficult to provide schools, water, housing and health services for so many people. Many young children – about 191 for every 1,000 babies born – die before they are five years old because they do not receive basic health care.

HIV/AIDS

HIV/AIDS is a serious health problem in Nigeria. In 2011 AIDS killed about 210,000 Nigerians. About another 3.5 million people have the HIV virus, which could lead to AIDS. The Nigerian government is trying to tackle this disease by providing drugs and teaching people how to avoid getting HIV/AIDS. The drugs cannot cure HIV/AIDS, but they can control it.

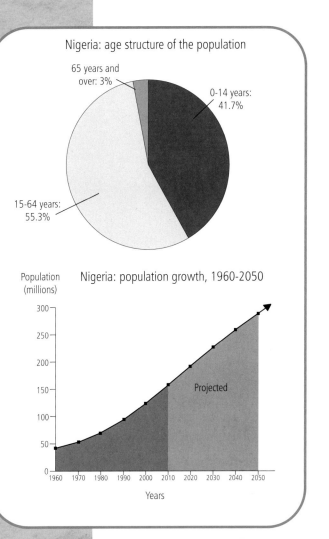

Nigeria: age structure of the population

65 years and over: 3%

0-14 years: 41.7%

15-64 years: 55.3%

Nigeria: population growth, 1960-2050

Population (millions)

Projected

Years

DID YOU KNOW?

The United Nations estimates that by the year 2050 Nigeria's population will have doubled – to 289 million people.

▶ In some places in Nigeria there is a free health service scheme. Even so, most hospitals do not have enough staff or equipment to meet demand.

Settlements and living

Nigeria is rapidly becoming a country where most people live in towns and cities. The number of people living in urban areas is rising rapidly, by about 1 per cent every two years.

Life in the country

In rural Nigeria, people live in villages in small houses usually grouped together in compounds. Most daily activities, such as cooking and washing, are done outside. Usually the houses have no indoor plumbing or electricity. Most people are farmers. When they are old enough, many young people leave villages with high hopes of finding work in towns and cities.

Facts at a glance

Urban population: 49.8% (78.8 million)

Rural population: 50.2% (79.4 million)

Population of largest city: 21 million (Lagos)

A boy living in northern Nigeria herds cattle. He is part of the Fulani ethnic group, who travel from place to place looking after their livestock.

Towns and cities

Nigeria's towns and cities are growing quickly. They have mostly grown in an unplanned way. Shanty towns have sprung up where people have built their own homes, with no piped water or electricity. New housing estates have been built in many other places.

Nigeria's cities

Nigeria has eleven cities with a population of more than 750,000, including Benin City (1.3 million), Port Harcourt (1.1 million) and Ibadan (2.8 million) in the south and Kano (3.4 million) and Kaduna (1.5 million) in the north.

Lagos, a coastal city in south-west Nigeria, is by far the country's largest city. Lagos is an important port and the home of several universities and colleges. Although it has slums and shanty towns, it also has areas of good housing where rich people live.

Lagos has a high crime rate. Wealthy people usually live in walled compounds and employ guards for protection. The population of Lagos is growing by more than 250,000 people each year.

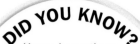

DID YOU KNOW? Kano, in northern Nigeria, is believed to be the oldest settlement in West Africa. Tools have been discovered here which indicate that people lived here more than 1,500 years ago.

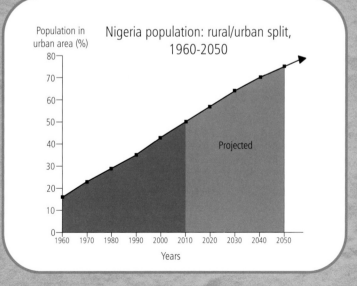

Population in urban area (%)

Nigeria population: rural/urban split, 1960-2050

Projected

Years

◬ Middle-class housing is set apart from poor areas of Nigeria.

Family life

The family is very important to Nigerians and is at the heart of Nigerian life. But many traditional aspects of family life are changing as Nigerians adopt more Western, urban lifestyles.

Families

Traditionally Nigerians lived in extended families, with parents, children, grandparents and other relatives living together or very close to one another. As more people move to cities, it is becoming more common for only parents and children to live together. Nigerians still have a strong sense of family though and often refer to even distant cousins as 'brother' or 'sister'.

Facts at a glance

Average children per childbearing woman:
5 children

Average household size:
4.9 people

A Hausa family relaxes at home. Looking after children is the responsibility of women in Nigeria.

It is common for Nigerian families to have five or six children. In Muslim families and some other groups in Nigeria, a man may have as many as four wives, as long as he can afford to keep them. However, it is becoming less common for a man to have as many as four wives.

Family celebrations

Nigerians often mark an occasion with a big party. Weddings and naming ceremonies are special times when an extended family comes together, often travelling long distances. There is always plenty of food, music and dancing. Many Nigerians like the opportunity to show others what they can afford by holding lavish parties.

Women's role

The role of women is changing in Nigeria, especially those who live in the cities. Increasingly they go out to work in offices or shops. Some go to university and work as lawyers and in businesses – jobs they would not have done 30 years ago. In rural areas women might grow vegetables and sell them in the market. But wherever they are and whatever they do, women are often still responsible for looking after the home and children. Nigerians increasingly realise the importance of school for girls, but traditional Muslim groups in the north often limit what girls and women can do.

◬ Nigerian family members gather together to celebrate important events such as weddings.

DID YOU KNOW?
In the Yoruba culture, women are usually known by the name of their firstborn child with the word 'mama' in front of it.

Religion and beliefs

Many people in Nigeria are religious. About half the country are Muslims, 40 per cent are Christian and the rest follow traditional beliefs. It is common to find Nigerians of all religions celebrating the main Christian and Islamic festivals.

Islam from the north

More than a thousand years ago, traders came across the Sahara Desert from North Africa, and brought Islam to the people in northern Nigeria. Ethnic groups such as the Hausa and Fulani, and some Yorubas, are Muslim. They take part in Muslim religious events, such as fasting during the month of Ramadan. This month is followed by the feast of *Id-ul-Fitr*.

Several Muslim-dominated states in the north have tried to bring in *Sharia*, or Islamic law. This has resulted in protests from Nigerians of other religions who do not want to have to follow another religion's laws.

DID YOU KNOW?

According to a BBC report in 2004, Nigeria is the most religious nation in the world. More than 90 per cent of Nigerians said they believed in a god.

▼ Worshippers gather at the prayer ground of the main mosque in the northern city of Kano.

Christianity

European missionaries visited the south part of Nigeria in the nineteenth century. They converted many Nigerians from the traditional beliefs they held to Christianity. Today church services are often celebrated with music, clapping and dancing. Christmas is a time when Christian Nigerians – even those living abroad – come home to spend time with their extended family. Christmas is celebrated across the country, although not as much in the north where there are fewer Christians.

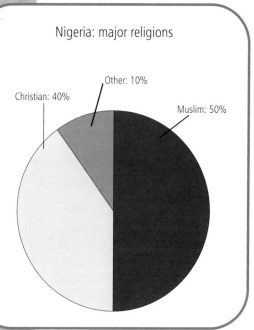

Nigeria: major religions

Other: 10%

Christian: 40%

Muslim: 50%

Traditional beliefs

In addition to following Islam or Christianity, many Nigerians also follow traditional beliefs, often at the same time. According to these beliefs everything in nature has a soul. In ceremonies some people wear masks to represent their ancestors. People believe that they can then act as go-betweens so that the dead ancestors can 'visit' the land of the living. Once this has happened they can be asked to help cure someone who is sick, help with the harvest or help set up a new business.

◀ Every year on 26 December, children parade in the streets of Calabar in south-east Nigeria. The street carnival is part of Christmas celebrations.

Education and learning

Although children in Nigeria are required to go to primary school, only about three-quarters do so. Parents cannot always afford the books and uniforms they need to buy to send their children to school. Some children, especially girls, are kept at home to help with the housework.

Primary school

Most children start school when they are six years old. At first they are taught in their local language, but after a couple of years they are taught in English. Classes are large, with up to forty students in one class. Nigerian students must pass an exam before they go to secondary school. If they do not pass they may have to stay at primary school for another year, or until they do pass. In the north, some boys go to *madrassas* – special Muslim schools – where they learn the Qur'an, the Muslim holy book, off by heart.

Secondary school

Facts at a glance

Children in primary school:
Male 72%, Female 64%

Children in secondary school:
Male 29%, Female 25%

Literacy rate (over 15 years):
61.3%

▶ This Muslim girl is reading from the Qur'an. Children in Islamic schools learn at least one chapter of the Qur'an off by heart before they are six years old.

Secondary school

Only one-third of Nigerian children go on to secondary school. Many leave to work or because the parents cannot afford it. Although there are some good schools, especially private ones in the cities, most are in very poor condition. There are not enough trained teachers, books or equipment, and school buildings are often very run-down. Those who can afford it often prefer to send their children abroad to stay with relatives in the UK or US so that they can go to schools there. Successful students may go on to one of Nigeria's 36 universities, which also attract students from all over West Africa.

Learning at home

In Nigerian villages many children learn traditional skills from their parents and other adults. They learn how to farm and are told stories about the history of their family and ancestors. These stories are told from one generation to another and are known as an oral tradition.

▼ Computer skills are becoming increasingly important in the Nigerian school curriculum.

DID YOU KNOW?

There are more than 18 million students in Nigeria at all levels. That is more than the school population of France, Britain and Spain combined.

17

Employment and economy

Nigeria has two economies – a modern one based on the money the country earns from oil, and a traditional one based on farming and trading. While the majority of the Nigerian workforce is involved in farming, oil brings in most of the money.

The importance of oil

Nigeria's economy is largely dependent on oil. Ninety five per cent of all the money Nigeria makes from exports comes from selling its oil. In the past the Nigerian government has failed to use this money to a build the country in a way where everyone can benefit. Much of

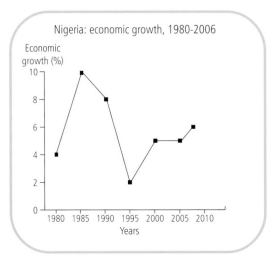

Nigeria: economic growth, 1980-2006

Economic growth (%)

▼ Employees work at an oil station in the Niger Delta region of Nigeria.

Facts at a glance

Contributions to GDP:
agriculture: 30.9%
industry: 43%
services: 26%

Labour force:
agriculture: 70%
industry: 10%
services: 20%

Female labour force:
42.8% of total

Unemployment rate: 24%

23

Members of the government accepted bribes from large foreign oil companies such as Mobil, Chevron and Shell. In return the government awarded them contracts to drill for oil in Nigeria.

Today the Nigerian government is trying to reform the country's economy. Although the oil companies employ many Nigerians, they often do not give them top-level jobs. Many people believe that Nigerians should be trained for these jobs. They feel that the oil companies should help Nigerians by building hospitals and schools.

Unemployment and the informal sector

Many adults and children in Nigeria work in what is called the informal sector. This is where someone works on a casual basis and there is no record of them working. Informal workers often do not pay taxes on the money they earn. In Lagos many people work in the informal sector. For example, they may sell water in the streets or shine shoes in the hotels.

The brain drain

Every year thousands of young people leave Nigeria. Some leave to study at colleges and universities, and some leave to find work abroad, mainly to the UK and US. Many of those who leave, such as doctors and teachers, have skills and talents that would be useful to Nigeria.

DID YOU KNOW? In 2008 Nigerians working abroad sent US$10 billion back home to their families. This money is an important source of income for many Nigerian families.

▶ Pot making is a traditional industry in parts of Nigeria. The special pots, usually made by women, keep water cool.

Industry and trade

Nigeria is rich in mineral and energy resources. Foreign money and investment is needed to help develop these resources in Nigeria. However, careful management is needed so that foreign companies do not take advantage of Nigeria's resources.

'Bonny Light'

Nigeria's oil reserves are bigger than those of the US and Mexico combined. They are estimated at 36.2 billion barrels, enough oil to last another 30 years if people continue to extract it at the same rate. A special oil known as 'Bonny Light' is found in Nigeria. It is easy to refine into gasoline and diesel and is therefore in high demand around the world.

DID YOU KNOW?

Nigeria has its own film industry. Nearly 2,000 films are produced each year on DVD and are shown in small video clubs and homes all over Nigeria, as well as other African countries.

▼ Most of Nigeria's imports and exports pass through the port of Lagos, the largest in Nigeria.

Resources and energy

Nigeria has many mineral resources, including coal, iron ore and limestone. It has reserves of columbite, which is used in the making of mobile phones. It also has uranium, lead, zinc, tungsten and gold. However, the mining industry is not well developed and needs more investment in order to bring in a good profit. Nigeria itself does not have the money to put into mining. It needs help raising this money from foreign companies and governments.

Most of Nigeria's energy is produced from oil, while about 35 per cent of its energy comes from natural gas and 8 per cent comes from hydroelectricity.

Manufacturing

Nigeria is ranked third in Africa in the amount of goods made in its factories. About 8 per cent of Nigeria's work force is employed here. They manufacture food products, leather shoes, clothes, cigarettes and soap. Many international companies have set up their own factories in Nigeria to make products such as soft drinks and processed food.

Trading partners

Nigeria is a member of ECOWAS (the Economic Community of West African States). This is a collection of fifteen countries that support one another to develop economically. Nigeria also trades with the US, Brazil and Spain. They buy most of Nigeria's exports, especially its oil. Nigeria buys machinery, chemicals, transport equipment, manufactured goods and food from China, the Netherlands, the US, South Korea, the UK and others.

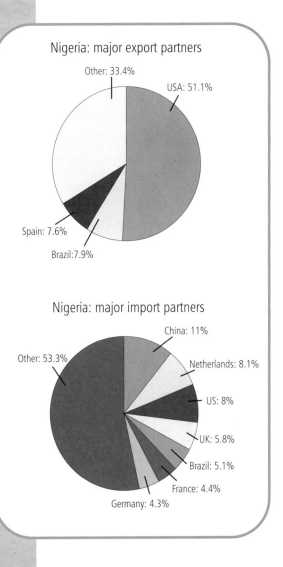

Nigeria: major export partners

Other: 33.4%
USA: 51.1%
Spain: 7.6%
Brazil: 7.9%

Nigeria: major import partners

China: 11%
Netherlands: 8.1%
US: 8%
UK: 5.8%
Brazil: 5.1%
France: 4.4%
Germany: 4.3%
Other: 53.3%

▼ Tin is another important mineral in Nigeria. Africa's main tin-producing region is the Jos Plateau, in north-central Nigeria.

Farming and food

In the 1960s Nigeria was able to produce all the food it needed. During an oil boom in the 1970s, Nigeria started to import a lot of foreign food. Today it still has to import food, particularly processed foods like pasta, biscuits and tinned food. Nigeria buys US$459.5 million worth of wheat from the US every year.

Farming today

Seventy per cent of Nigerians are farmers and most of these are subsistence farmers. They produce enough food for themselves and their family and if there is any left over it is sold at the market or to wholesalers. Farmers grow cassava, corn, palm oil, peanuts, sorghum and yams.

Crops such as cocoa and rubber are produced for export on large, mainly foreign-owned plantations but contribute less than 5 per cent to Nigeria's exports.

DID YOU KNOW?
The Yam Festival is one of the most important Nigerian festivals. It is usually held at the beginning of August and is a celebration of the harvesting of the yam.

◀ These women weed their crops frequently. Between 60 and 80 per cent of the farmers in Nigeria are women.

Eating

Food is an important part of hospitality in Nigerian homes. Nigerians often cook more than enough in case they have an unexpected visitor. In the north, people enjoy drinking tea while they sit together and talk. Generally Nigerians enjoy spicy, peppery food, cooked in palm oil and eaten with rice, although each area has its own regional food.

Nigerians enjoy stews and soups with dumplings, which they might eat with something called *fufu*, otherwise known as mashed yams. People who live near the coast eat stews made from seafood, yams, rice and vegetables. Meat is more popular in the north than in the south. Fruits, such as oranges, mangos, melons, pineapples and bananas, are available nearly everywhere.

Fast food

Traditionally Nigerians buy their food in open markets. However, in towns and cities, it is becoming more common to go to supermarkets or buy fast food from a 'chop bar' (a food stall) or a street vendor selling dishes such as ukwaka (a steamed pudding made from corn and ripe plantains), and moin-moin, (a steamed cake of ground dried beans and fish). These dishes may be served with jollof rice (a spicy tomato-based rice), cassava, yams, okra, beans, plantains, or kebabs (sticks of lamb or beef grilled over a fire).

◗ A woman carries baskets of food at an outdoor market in Lagos.

Facts at a glance

Farmland: 37% of total land area

Main agricultural exports: Cocoa beans, rubber, cocoa butter

Main agricultural imports: Wheat, rice, powdered milk

Average daily calorie intake: 2,700 calories

Transport and communications

Being able to travel around easily is important to help a country trade and for people to be able to work in different places. However, Nigeria's roads and railways are in a poor state of repair. The government is now trying to improve and modernise the transport system as it knows how important this is – but this will take about 25 years.

Getting around

Many people who live in villages rarely leave their villages and tend to walk when they need to go somewhere. People travelling between towns and cities usually go by car or taxi, often sharing with others, or by bus.

Facts at a glance

Total roads: 193,200 km (120,049 miles)

Paved roads: 28,980 km (18,007 miles)

Railways: 3,505 km (2,178 miles)

Major airports: 18

Major ports: 3

▼ Unpaved roads, such as in Port Harcourt, are common in rural areas as well as in cities.

The journeys are often very bumpy and slow as the roads are full of potholes caused by heavy downpours during the rainy season. Traffic in the cities is also slow because there is so much congestion. Bicycles and motorbike taxis known as *okadas* are popular ways of getting around.

Railways

Nigeria needs railways to transport its resources to the ports of Lagos, Calabar and Port Harcourt and so people can travel around the country quickly and easily. But Nigeria's railway system is old. It was originally built by the British over a hundred years ago with two lines running from the north to the south. Today it has more than 3,500 kilometres (2,175 miles) of track, but it has been largely neglected.

⊙ The city of Lagos is spread over four islands connected by a system of bridges. For many people, the daily rush-hour commute to work is on foot.

DID YOU KNOW?

China, one of Nigeria's import partners, has given US$8 billion to help Nigeria build a railway between Lagos and Kano. The railway will move goods and people between the two cities.

Going mobile

The system of landline phones in Nigeria has never been reliable. When mobile phones became available in 2000, their use mushroomed. In 2008 more mobile phones were sold in Nigeria than in any other African country. Everywhere you go you can see street vendors selling mobiles and selling top-up cards. Internet cafes are commonplace and the ownership of personal computers is on the rise. In 2013 there were 56 million Internet subscribers in Nigeria, a number that has been rising rapidly.

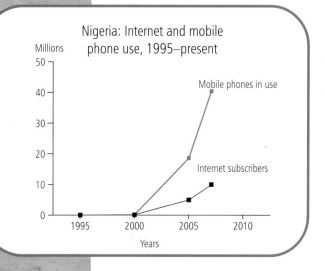

Nigeria: Internet and mobile phone use, 1995–present

Millions

Mobile phones in use

Internet subscribers

Years

Leisure and tourism

Sports of all kinds, music and films are popular pastimes in Nigeria. The country has good beaches and beautiful scenery. Its sanctuaries and parks are a destination for bird watching and wildlife safaris.

Sport

Nigeria's athletes excel across the world in football, basketball, boxing (it has had three world champions) and sprinting. Its football team – the Super Eagles – reached the finals of the World Cup in 2002. In the Beijing Olympics in 2008, Nigeria won a silver medal in football, a bronze in taekwondo, and two bronzes in women's athletics. Nigeria also took part in wrestling, boxing, weightlifting, tennis and table tennis at the Games.

DID YOU KNOW?
Many Nigerian footballers have played in the English Premier Football League, including John Obi Mikel for Chelsea and Joseph Yobo for Everton.

Music

Music accompanies any Nigerian social event. Modern hip hop, juju and apala music, mixed with Jamaican reggae and other traditional rhythms, are popular in the nightclubs of towns and cities.

▶ Ebenezer Ajilore of Nigeria shoots the ball during a football match at the Beijing Olympic Games in August 2008.

Traditional music, played on drums and flutes, remains popular in villages and at traditional ceremonies such as weddings. Modern music is also popular with young people in Kano in the north.

Watching Nigerian films on DVD in video clubs all over the country is very popular. Nigerian films are usually stories about what people do when they are in difficult situations and how they get on with other people. The films are made in Hausa, Yoruba and Igbo as well as in English.

Tourism

Tourism in Nigeria mainly attracts visitors from other West African countries. Because Nigeria's roads are poor and there is a lot of visible poverty and crime, it is likely to be many years before Nigeria can fully develop its tourist industry.

Facts at a glance

Tourist arrivals (millions)

Year	Arrivals
1995	0.7
2000	0.8
2005	1.0
2010	1.5

Filmmaking is a big industry in Nigeria. It employs more than 300,000 people there.

Environment and wildlife

Nigeria has one of the worst environmental records in the world. Deforestation, oil pollution and the advance of the deserts are the main problems it faces. Despite its problems, Nigeria is home to a wide variety of wildlife that includes gorillas, chimpanzees, baboons, elephants, birds, reptiles and nearly five thousand different species of plants.

Losing land

The habitats of many animals and fertile land have been lost over the last few decades to the development of towns. Animals such as lions and leopards that used to roam freely are now often only to be seen in sanctuaries and wildlife parks.

In the north, the desert is advancing by about 600 m (2,000 ft) each year. Farmers are losing fertile land and being forced to abandon their farms.

Facts at a glance

Proportion of area protected: 3.6%

Biodiversity (known species): 5,904

Threatened species: 204

▼ Dust storms frequently occur in areas where the deserts are advancing.

Oil and the environment

The development of the oil industry has created challenges for the Niger Delta. Whilst the oil brings in money for the country, the drilling of it has meant that good farmland has been used up, and the creeks and streams have become polluted.

Environmental organisations such as Friends of the Earth International think the oil companies should pay for the damage they do the environment. Nigeria's government is beginning to take notice of the environmental problems and is taking action. They are trying to stop the cutting down of trees and are replanting new ones. But there is a very long way to go to make up for the destruction of the last 100 years.

◯ Oil company workers clean up an oil spill from an abandoned well.

DID YOU KNOW?
Lake Chad, in the north-east of Nigeria is now one-twentieth the size it was in the 1960s. It has lost water because of increasing demands for water for irrigation and decreasing rainfall.

Glossary

abroad away from one's home in a foreign country

ancestors people you are descended from, before your grandparents

bribes sums of money offered in exchange for something

cash crop crop which can be bought and sold for money

colonies countries controlled by other countries

compound a collection of buildings where members of the same family usually live

deforestation the loss of forests due to cutting down trees

delta where a river meets the sea and spreads out, forming lots of islands

democracy a form of government where people elect people to represent them

desert an area of very dry land that has very little rainfall

desertification the loss of habitable land into desert

drought a shortage of rainfall

export good or service that is sold to another country

extended family members of a family beyond mother, father and their children

GDP the total value of goods and services produced by a country

habitats the places where animals and plants live and exist

iron ore a rock from which iron can be extracted

HIV/AIDS stands for Human Immunodeficiency Virus/Acquired Immune Deficiency Syndrome

humid a high level of moisture in the air

hydroelectricity electricity produced by water power

import good or service that is bought from another country

independence freedom from control or influence of another country

irrigation a system of ditches and channels made to provide water to dry land

mangrove a type of tree that grows on muddy coasts with long roots, some of which grow above ground

missionaries members of a religion who work to convert those who do not already share the same faith

mosque Muslim place of worship

naming ceremony a ceremony at which a baby is given a name, usually a week after he or she is born

natural resources naturally occurring things found in land, air or water which are useful to human beings

oral tradition the spoken stories, from one generation to the next, of a people's cultural history and ancestry

raw materials resources such as timber and oil that are used to make products or other materials

refine to remove the impurities from oil

Sharia Islamic law based on the Qur'an

shanty towns settlements (sometimes illegal or unauthorized) of poor people who live in improvised dwellings made from scrap materials

sorghum tropical cereal grass

subsistence farming farming that provides for the basic needs of the farmer

tropical the area between the Tropic of Cancer and the Tropic of Capricorn

watershed a ridge of land that separates two adjacent river systems

wetlands a lowland area, such as a marsh or swamp, that is saturated with moisture,

Topic web

Use this topic web to explore Nigerian themes in different areas of your curriculum.

History
The Benin Empire existed in Nigeria for more than 400 years. Find ten facts about the Benin Empire.

Geography
Look through the photos in this book. Make a list of the things you think are similar to the UK and things you think are different. For example, how people live, the jobs they do and their religions and cultures.

Science
Make a list of minerals found in Nigeria. Include a description for each mineral listed.

Maths
Work out approximately how many times the UK would fit into Nigeria.

Nigeria

ICT
Use a search engine such as Google and find a recipe for a typical Nigerian dish, such as jollof rice. Find out how to say 'hello' in Yoruba, Hausa and Igbo.

Design and Technology
Mask-making is an important art form in Nigeria. Design and make your own mask.

Citizenship
Make a list of all the ways in which the UK and Nigeria are connected. Think of food, music and trade.

English
Imagine you are on holiday in Nigeria. Write a postcard home describing something you saw or did on your holiday.

Further information and index

Further reading

Nigeria (The Changing Face of...) by Rob Bowden and Roy Maconachie (Wayland 2006)

Nigeria (World in Focus) Ali Brownlie Bojang (Wayland 2009)

West Africa (Festivals and Food) Ali Brownlie Bojang (Wayland 2006)

Web

http://news.bbc.co.uk/1/hi/world/africa/country_profiles/1064557.stm

This is the BBC news page for Nigeria, with recent events and background information.

www.timeforkids.com/TFK/kids/hh/goplaces/main/0,28375,1044380,00.html

This web page takes its visitors on a 'virtual voyage' across Nigeria, exploring the country's wildlife, history and facts.

Index